PATHWAY
4949 Fulton Rd., N.W.
Canton, OH 447

MW01520956

ACCESSING FEDERAL ADOPTION SUBSIDIES AFTER LEGALIZATION

Tim O'Hanlon Ph.D.

Child Welfare League of America

Washington, DC

© 1995 by the Child Welfare League of America, Inc.

All rights reserved. Neither this book nor any part may be reproduced or transmitted in any form or by any means, electronic or mechanical, including photocopying, microfilming, and recording, or by any information storage and retrieval system, without permission in writing from the publisher. For information on this or other CWLA publications, contact the CWLA Publications Department at the address below.

CHILD WELFARE LEAGUE OF AMERICA, INC.
440 First Street, NW, Suite 310, Washington, DC 20001-2085

CURRENT PRINTING (last digit)
10 9 8 7 6 5 4 3 2 1

Cover and text design by Jennifer Riggs-Geanakos

Printed in the United States of America

ISBN # 0–87868–569–3

CONTENTS

INTRODUCTION

Recent changes in the federal Title IV-E adoption assistance program provide an opportunity for adoptive families who are struggling to meet the medical and psychological needs of their children to receive badly needed financial and medical assistance. Families who adopted children without provision for adoption assistance (subsidy) may now file an appeal for a reconsideration of their child's eligibility for the federal Title IV-E adoption assistance program.* Children who are found to be eligible can receive financial support and Medicaid benefits and their parents may petition for retroactive adoption assistance payments as part of their appeal.

The state's administrative fair hearing system provides this new venue of appeal. Parents who wish to petition for adoption assistance after a final decree of adoption should be able to obtain an administrative fair hearing in virtually every case where information relevant to the child's eligibility was not available to the adoptive family prior to the adoption.

This guide is designed to help adoptive families apply for adoption assistance after legalization of their child's adoption and for retroactive adoption assistance payments, regardless of the family's state of residence. Chapter one provides a brief history of the changes in policy. In chapter two, a question and answer format is used to walk adoptive parents and agency

---

* The terms *adoption assistance* and *adoption subsidy* are used interchangeably throughout the text, unless a specific program such as Title IV-E adoption assistance is being discussed.

professionals through the appeals process and issues stemming from changes in federal policy. These question and answers are followed by a discussion in chapter 3 of the costs and benefits of providing retroactive adoption assistance payments to adoptive families with special-needs children. Chapter 4 addresses typical anxieties and obstacles faced by parents when they attempt to secure postadoption services for their children. Suggestions are also offered to help agency professionals become more responsive to the needs of adoptive families and assist adoptive parents in becoming more effective advocates for their children. Finally, the appendix provides copies of the key federal policy decisions and a list of information resources.

1 THE CHANGE IN TITLE IV-E ADOPTION ASSISTANCE POLICY

The seminal Adoption Assistance and Child Welfare Act of 1980 created the Title IV-E adoption assistance program to provide financial support, medical assistance, and other services to families adopting children with special needs. Over the years, the program has both encouraged and sustained the adoption of children who might otherwise wait years in out-of-home care. Time inevitably reveals defects in the best of social programs, however, and Title IV-E is no exception. Until recently, the program was hampered in meeting its intended purpose by federal regulations that required the completion of a written agreement for adoption assistance *prior to* the final decree of adoption.

Because special needs are often developmental in nature, an array of medical and emotional problems may be latent at the time of a child's adoption. Unexpected problems that arise can quickly escalate and exhaust adoptive families' budgets and health insurance. When adoptive parents faced a crisis and contacted state agencies for help, they were informed that assistance was not available if the adoption had been finalized. In 1988, however, a federal policy interpretation—PIQ 88-06*— provided a ray of hope for the adoptive families and advocates struggling to remove this regulatory impediment to obtaining adoption assistance

Although there have been few changes in federal law or

---

* PIQ 88-06 is reprinted in appendix A.

regulations pertaining to the Title IV-E adoption assistance program, interpretations and policy issues have been addressed through periodic statements known as Policy Interpretation Questions (PIQs), published by the Children's Bureau at the U.S. Department of Health and Human Services. In PIQ 88-06, federal officials indicated for the first time that exceptions could be made to the regulation requiring that adoption assistance be arranged prior to legalization.

The case prompting the policy interpretation involved a Tennessee family who could not verify their child's special-needs condition until after the final decree of adoption. PIQ 88-06 indicated that the child's eligibility for adoption assistance could be reconsidered *if* an administrative fair hearing established that "all of the facts relevant to the child's eligibility were not presented at the time of the request for assistance."

This federal policy announcement had potentially far-reaching implications for struggling adoptive families. Although it raised more questions than it answered, PIQ 88-06 identified the state's administrative fair hearing system as the vehicle for case-by-case reconsideration of eligibility for adoption assistance, thereby providing a direction for reform efforts.

On June 25, 1992, in the midst of a growing effort being waged by adoptive families, child advocates, and some states to open up access to adoption assistance after legalization, the Children's Bureau issued the landmark PIQ 92-02,* entitled *Fair Hearing and Extenuating Circumstances.* This policy announcement addressed many of the questions left unanswered by PIQ 88-06. While it did not formally change the federal rule requiring adoption assistance be arranged prior to finalization, PIQ 92-02 authorized a procedure by which case-by-case exceptions may be made if adoptive parents demonstrate that extenuating circumstances prevented them from applying for adoption assistance or completing an adoption assistance agreement prior to legalization.

PIQ 92-02 reiterated PIQ 88-06's stipulation that applica-

---

* PIQ 92-02 is reprinted in appendix A.

tions for adoption assistance after a final decree of adoption must be considered through the state's administrative fair hearing system or other administrative appeals process. The new policy interpretation also made states eligible to receive federal reimbursement if they award retroactive adoption assistance to eligible children and families.

At the administrative fair hearing, the primary burden on adoptive families is to show that circumstances for which they were not responsible, such as a lack of pertinent information about the child or about subsidy programs, prevented them from applying for or establishing adoption assistance prior to the final decree of adoption. When successful, such arguments should lead to a reexamination of the child's eligibility for Title IV-E adoption assistance.

Implementation of PIQ 92-02 by the states has been inconsistent. In September 1992, Ohio became one of the first states to set forth regulations for reconsideration of a child's eligibility for adoption assistance after finalization, and by December, 1993, had effected rules awarding retroactive adoption assistance payments to most children who become eligible for adoption assistance after finalization. At the other end of the spectrum, a number of states have done little or nothing to implement PIQ 92-02, even though more than two and a half years have passed since the policy change was issued. Underscoring this point, a study released in August 1994, by the North American Council on Adoptable Children found that two out of three public adoption workers surveyed were not even aware that it was possible to obtain federal adoption assistance after legalization of an adoption.

2 OBTAINING ADOPTION ASSISTANCE: QUESTIONS AND ANSWERS

Although specific procedures and regulations differ from state to state, all state policies for awarding adoption assistance after a final decree of adoption should embrace certain common principles to be in compliance with federal law.

1. Adoptive families have basic due process rights. Families who have adopted a child have a right to appeal for a reconsideration of the child's eligibility for Title IV-E adoption assistance through the state's administrative fair hearing system. A state cannot simply refuse to reconsider the child's application or deny access to the fair hearing system merely because the adoption has been legalized.

2. States must define the "extenuating circumstances" that will lead to a redetermination of the child's eligibility for Title IV-E adoption assistance. The state's definition of extenuating circumstances cannot be more restrictive than the list presented in PIQ 92-02 (see appendix A).

3. States have an affirmative responsibility to inform agencies and adoptive families about the opportunity to appeal for a reconsideration of Title IV-E adoption assistance after legalization of the adoption.

Part 1 of the questions and answers that follow pertains to obtaining federal adoption assistance after a final decree of adoption, part 2 addresses retroactive adoption assistance payments, part 3 provides information relevant to appealing adverse decisions, and part 4 provides a summary.

Part 1
Obtaining Adoption Assistance After a Final Decree

Getting Started

What kinds of benefits can adoptive parents secure for their child if they succeed in establishing the child's eligibility for adoption assistance after legalization of the adoption?

Children whose eligibility has been established after legalization of their adoptions are eligible for the same future benefits as if the final decree of adoption had not yet taken place, namely:

- A negotiated amount of monthly financial assistance,
- Medicaid coverage, and
- Title XX social services (as available).

Adoptive parents also have the opportunity to pursue retroactive adoption assistance payments (see part 2, below).

Must an adoptive family appeal through the state's administrative fair hearing system* in order to obtain adoption assistance after a final decree of adoption?

Federal regulations requiring that an adoption assistance agreement be completed *before* a final decree of adoption are still in effect. Federal Policy Interpretation Questions (PIQ) 88-06 and 92-02, however, authorized a means by which case-by-case exceptions may be made. The adoptive parents must demonstrate, through an administrative hearing process, that extenuating circumstances prevented them from applying for adoption assistance or completing an adoption assistance agreement prior to legalization of the adoption.

The right to an administrative fair hearing for applicants

---

* In some states, the process is called an *administrative fair hearing*, in others, an *administrative hearing*. The terms are used interchangeably throughout this book.

and recipients of federal assistance programs was affirmed in 1970 by the U.S. Supreme Court in *Goldberg v. Kelly*. Traditionally, administrative fair hearing appeals have focused on eligibility issues pertaining to public assistance programs such as AFDC. In recent years, however, adoptive families have used the administrative hearing system to bring about major reforms in Title IV-E adoption assistance policy.

How do adoptive parents file an appeal and obtain a hearing? Adoptive parents should file their appeal for adoption assistance in the state containing the public or private agency that held custody or guardianship of their adopted child after the rights of the child's biological parents were terminated and that was responsible for placing the child for adoption. Eligibility and application procedures for intercountry and nonagency adoptions are discussed below.

Parents should contact the adoption section in the state's department of human services and explain that they finalized the adoption of their special-needs child in 19___ and are interested in filing an appeal for Title IV-E adoption assistance. They should inform the state official that they are aware of federal PIQ 92-02 and the requirement that the child's eligibility must be established through an administrative fair hearing and should ask where and how to obtain that hearing. Parents should also request any written regulations or guidelines on the subject, as well as copies of current and past eligibility requirements for adoption subsidy programs.

Adoptive parents should not be discouraged if state or county officials tell them that it is not possible to obtain adoption assistance after legalization of their child's adoption or if they cannot obtain sufficient information because the state does not yet have clear guidelines on filing an appeal for adoption assistance after legalization.

The specific steps for filing an appeal for adoption assistance after a final decree of adoption may vary from state to state, but adoptive parents should be able to rely on certain basic due process rights to obtain a fair hearing.

The right to an administrative fair hearing is triggered by the denial of a federal benefit. If no other avenue exists, adoptive parents should be able to receive such a hearing by *filing an application for Title IV-E adoption assistance with the state or county agency to which they actually applied or should have applied for subsidy prior to the adoption.* They should keep a copy of the application they submit to the agency. If no application form is available, adoptive parents can petition for adoption assistance by submitting a letter to the state or county agency. The letter should include:

1. A statement making it clear that the purpose of the letter is to apply for Title IV-E adoption assistance through the appeal procedures outlined in PIQ 92–02.

2. A statement indicating when the final decree of adoption was issued and the family's current situation.

3. An explanation of the extenuating circumstances that prevented the parents from applying for adoption assistance or the child from being determined to be eligible for adoption assistance prior to legalization of the adoption.

4. A statement asking the agency to consider the letter both an application for the Title IV-E adoption assistance program and a request for an administrative fair hearing to determine the child's eligibility for the program.

Adoptive parents should not be surprised if their request for assistance is denied because the adoption has been legalized. Without some form of hearing procedure, states do not have the authority to establish adoption assistance after a final decree of adoption. They may not, however, completely ignore an application or letter requesting adoption assistance. Under federal law, adoptive parents are entitled to a written response to their request. That response should contain information about the right to appeal negative decisions and instructions on how to request a fair hearing.

If the state or agency fails to respond to the parents' application or letter within 30 to 45 days, or if the response does not contain sufficient information about the appeal process, adoptive parents should contact the state's office of administrative fair hearings for guidance. Unresponsiveness to an application is itself grounds for an administrative fair hearing. The office of administrative fair hearings is usually located in the state's department of human services.

Is there any cost involved in filing an appeal for adoption assistance and obtaining an administrative fair hearing?
Administrative fair hearings are available at no cost. For a detailed discussion of fees for other reviews, see part 3 of this chapter, "Appealing the Administrative Hearing Decision."

The Hearing Process

What are administrative fair hearings like?
Administrative fair hearings are not formal trials, but are relatively informal proceedings in which adoptive parents and other appellants should have ample opportunity to present their case in their own words.

Should adoptive parents be represented by legal counsel at the administrative fair hearing?
Adoptive parents are not required to have an attorney or other legal counsel present at the hearing. The decision to hire an attorney depends on a number of factors specific to each case, including family resources, how much is at stake in terms of the child's needs, and the complexity of the issues involved. Adoptive parents usually have a very good sense of the circumstances that prevented their child from receiving adoption assistance and are often their children's most eloquent advocates. In many cases, they are quite capable of effectively representing themselves at the hearing if they are well-informed about the policy issues and eligibility questions that must be addressed. The family also has the option of acquiring legal representation at a later stage of the process. For a further discussion of the value of legal counsel, see part 3 of this chapter, "Appealing the Administrative Hearing Decision."

Without detailed knowledge of a case, it is difficult to tell how much an adoptive family can benefit from securing legal counsel. One point is certain, however. Adoptive parents should never decline to participate in an administrative fair hearing because they cannot afford to hire an attorney. If the need for support exists, parents have little to lose by going forward with the appeal.

Before making a decision about whether to hire an attorney, it is advisable to consult with a local adoption support group to obtain a sense of the experiences of other families with administrative hearings in the state. Parents might also wish to contact one of the resource organizations listed in appendix B.

What kind of case should an adoptive family be prepared to make at an administrative fair hearing?

Adoptive parents must first establish that extenuating circumstances prevented them from applying for adoption assistance or prevented their child from being found eligible for adoption assistance. If they establish the existence of extenuating circumstances, then the child's eligibility for adoption assistance will be reconsidered. The parents may present written documentation, call on witnesses for oral testimony, or offer a combination of evidence and arguments.

Establishing Extenuating Circumstances

What kinds of extenuating circumstances might constitute grounds for a reconsideration of an adopted child's eligibility for adoption assistance after a final decree of adoption?

PIQ 92-02 lists several "types of situations" that would constitute extenuating circumstances:

1. Relevant facts regarding the child, the child's biological family, or the child's background were known but not presented to the adoptive parents prior to the legalization of the adoption.*

---

* For more information on disclosure of facts regarding the adoptive child, see DeWoody, M., *Adoption and disclosure: A review of the law* (Washington, DC: Child Welfare League of America, 1994).

2. The denial of assistance was based upon a means test of the adoptive family. According to federal law, the income of the adoptive family has no effect upon the child's eligibility for adoption assistance.

3. The state made an erroneous determination that the child was ineligible for adoption assistance.

4. The state or agency failed to advise the adoptive parents of the availability of adoption assistance.

Several significant court reviews of administrative hearing decisions leading up to PIQ 92-02 found that if the adoptive parents were never informed about the adoption assistance or subsidy programs, they could not reasonably be held accountable for failing to arrange adoption assistance for their child before the final decree of adoption. Following the issuance of PIQ 92-02, if parents establish at an administrative fair hearing that they were not informed about the subsidy programs, they can have their child's eligibility for adoption assistance redetermined. In many instances, agencies have been willing to support the adoptive parent's claim that they were not informed about adoption subsidy programs.

In addition to using the categories listed above, states also have considerable flexibility in determining if extenuating circumstances thwarted the intended purpose of the federal program by preventing otherwise eligible children from receiving the benefits they need. However, states may not adopt policies regarding grounds for a fair hearing or definitions of extenuating circumstances that are inconsistent with or more restrictive than federal policy.

What about cases in which the adoptive parents were unaware of the existence or the extent of the child's special needs until after the final decree of adoption. Would such situations fall under the heading of extenuating circumstances?
Although not explicitly discussed in PIQ 92-02, situations in which the adoptive parents are not aware of the existence or true severity of their child's special needs until after the final decree of adoption would seem to meet the test of extenuating circum-

stances *if* the adoptive family can make a case similar to the one in the example that follows:

> **Example:** The child was adopted before the age of one. An adoption subsidy was not seriously considered because the child appeared to be in a state of normal health. A few years later, the child began to develop medical or emotional problems that escalated as the child grew older. Eventually, these problems exhausted the family's health insurance. The family requested adoption assistance but the request was denied on the grounds that the adoption had been finalized.

To make their case for an extenuating circumstance, the parents might argue at the administrative fair hearing that:

1. The child's current special-needs condition is consistent with factors in the child's medical history or background. It is reasonable to conclude that the child's medical or psychological problems are due to genetic factors or are linked to events that occurred prior to the final decree of adoption. (The adoptive family should attempt to secure written diagnoses, written statements, or direct testimony from relevant professionals that establishes the strongest connection possible between the child's existing special needs and his or her preadoptive history.)

2. The child's special needs did not *originate* after the final decree of adoption, but were *discovered* after the adoption was finalized.

3. The Title IV-E adoption assistance program covers children with special needs such as those experienced by the child in question. To deny a reconsideration of the child's eligibility for adoption assistance would inflict a severe and unfair penalty on a family that adopted a child in good faith. Such a denial would hold the family responsible for knowledge that was not available to them at the time the adoption was legalized.

4. It is reasonable to conclude that the adoptive parents [and the agency] would have pursued adoption subsidy with

more vigor had they known the problems that were in store for the child.

5. Reconsideration of the child's eligibility in cases such as this one is consistent with the decision in PIQ 88-06, which described the successful appeal of a family who was unable to confirm a diagnosis of the juvenile rheumatoid arthritis affecting their child until after the adoption was completed. The PIQ justified reconsideration of eligibility after legalization of the adoption on the grounds that information relevant to the child's eligibility was not available at the time an application was submitted. In the present case, an application was not submitted precisely because knowledge relevant to the child's eligibility, namely the severity of the child's special needs, was not available.

Establishing Eligibility

What eligibility requirements must be met if the fair hearing determines that extenuating circumstances prevented the adoptive parents from applying for or receiving adoption assistance?

The state or authorized agency must determine that the child met the Title IV-E adoption assistance eligibility requirements prior to legalization of the adoption. The eligibility requirements include:

1. **Special Needs:** Federal law does not define *special needs* in terms of specific disabilities and circumstances. Rather, it lists general conditions (i.e., medical, emotional, physical, or mental problems) and circumstances (i.e., ethnic background, age, membership in a sibling group). This approach gives individual states considerable flexibility in determining if a specific disability, age, or other condition is sufficient to classify the child as having special needs.

In the typical appeals case, parents petition the state for adoption assistance after a final decree of adoption precisely because they are struggling to cope with the child's severe medical, emotional, physical, or mental problems. If the child had a problem prior to the adoption that eventually required intensive or ongoing treatment, then he or she probably will meet the state's special-needs definition.

It can also be argued that the child meets the standard of special needs if there is a reasonable link between the child's current problems and his or preadoptive history. In such cases, the contention once again would be that the special needs existed, but were not discovered until after the adoption, and that the passage of time has demonstrated that the child is a special-needs child. Older children, minority children, and children adopted as part of a sibling group also may be eligible for adoption assistance after legalization, particularly if they waited a long time in out-of-home care before they were placed and if efforts had to be made to recruit adoptive parents.

Adoptive families should ask the state's adoption unit to send them a copy of the state's definition of special needs in effect at the time of the adoption decree. Because experience has shown that problems often arise after the adoption has been legalized, many states have responded by taking a somewhat generous, inclusive approach in determining if a child meets the criteria for special needs. As a reflection of this philosophy, state or agency officials may see the child's preadoptive circumstances and needs in a different, more sympathetic, light when reconsidering the child's eligibility on appeal than would have been the case in the year when the adoption was finalized.

2. **SSI/AFDC Relatedness:** In addition to meeting the federal definition of special needs, the child must have

   - met the eligibility requirements for the supplemental security income (SSI) program prior to legalization of the adoption; or

   - been receiving AFDC payments or have been eligible to receive AFDC payments in the month a petition was filed with the court, or a voluntary agreement was signed by the biological mother that lead to the removal of the child from the home and the placement of the child in out-of-home care; or

- been receiving AFDC payments or have been eligible to receive AFDC payments in any of the six months preceding the month in which a petition was filed with the court, or a voluntary agreement was signed by the biological mother that lead to the removal of the child from the home and the placement of the child in out-of-home care.*

It is not sufficient to merely determine if the biological parent (or relative) was receiving AFDC payments on behalf of the child during the period in question. If no AFDC payments were made, the state or designated agency must make a conscientious effort to reconstruct the case in order to determine if the child would have been eligible for AFDC or SSI payments had the biological parent or specified relative completed an application. Incomplete evidence is not sufficient grounds to rule against a child's eligibility for AFDC. In such cases, eligibility is determined on the strength of the information that is available.

3. **Judicial Determination of Best Interest:** A judicial determination to the effect that removal of the child from the home, or the placement of the child, was in the child's best interest also must be made. Federal policy interpretations such as PIQ 87–05, along with discussions with officials at the U.S. Children's Bureau, Administration for Children, Youth and Families, U.S. Department of Health and Human Services, confirm that there are two general exceptions to the "judicial determination of best interest" requirement:

   - children who meet the eligibility requirements for SSI, and
   - children whose care is not the responsibility of the state,

---

* Item 21 of Federal Information Memorandum 85–25 instructs federal reviewers to consider the following questions when determining if the AFDC relatedness requirement was met. "Did the child receive AFDC in or for the month of initiation (filing) of court proceedings of month placement agreement was entered into? Or would the child have received AFDC in any month within six (6) months prior to initiation of court proceedings or month of agreement, if he had applied?"

and who are residing with relatives at the time the relatives file a petition to adopt them.

Who has the burden of proof for establishing the child's eligibility for adoption assistance at the administrative hearing?
At first glance, PIQ 92-02 would appear to place the burden of proof for establishing the child's eligibility on the shoulders of the adoptive parents. When analyzed in the broader context of federal adoption assistance law and the due process rights of adoptive parents, however, a somewhat different interpretation of PIQ 92-02 emerges.

The answer to question 7 on page 5 of PIQ 92–02 (see appendix A) states that federal law does not address the question of the burden of proof in any explicit sense, but notes, "We would expect states to conclude that the adoptive parents have the burden of proving extenuating circumstances and adoption assistance eligibility at a fair hearing." While it appears reasonable for the adoptive family to assume the burden for establishing extenuating circumstances, the parent's responsibility for establishing their child's eligibility for adoption assistance requires further explanation.

While federal law may not explicitly use the term *burden of proof* in discussing questions of eligibility, it makes clear that the state or local agency, not the applicant, is responsible for determining eligibility for federal programs, including Title IV-E adoption assistance. The applicant has the responsibility of providing information to facilitate the eligibility determination. In the case of adoptive families filing an appeal for adoption assistance, such information would most frequently involve the child's special needs.

In eligibility determinations that are made *prior to* finalization, the adoptive parents are not expected to assume the primary burden for establishing whether the child meets the AFDC relatedness requirement or whether a judicial determination of best interest was made. Those eligibility requirements pertain to the child's situation at the time he or she was removed from the home of the biological parents, a period before the adoptive family came on the scene and had any relationship with the child. The state or local agency assumes responsibility for gathering the facts necessary to determine if the AFDC relatedness and judicial determination of best interest standards are satisfied.

In discussing the burden of proof, PIQ 92–02 fails to distinguish between the state's responsibility for *conducting* eligibility determinations and the adoptive family's responsibility for *responding* to eligibility determinations. If the state contends that the child is not eligible for adoption assistance because he or she did not meet the AFDC relatedness requirement, for example, the adoptive family must be prepared to challenge that claim with evidence of its own. The state, however, still has the responsibility for presenting the reasons why the child did not meet the AFDC relatedness requirement.

The adoptive parents' right to due process, including the opportunity for an administrative fair hearing, arises from the state's denial of adoption assistance benefits. Such a denial presupposes that an eligibility determination has already been made. If such rights are afforded to adoptive families prior to the adoption, then they should be available to adoptive families who apply after the adoption is legalized. In the majority of cases, the adoptive family is filing an appeal precisely because an eligibility determination has never been made.

In light of the state's fundamental responsibility for making eligibility determinations and for presenting evidence to support those determinations, what follows is a reasonable interpretation of the adoptive parents' burden of proof:

1. The establishment of extenuating circumstances constitutes grounds for determination or reconsideration of the child's eligibility for adoption assistance. Adoptive parents have a right to an administrative fair hearing if a benefit is denied. They should be able to obtain a hearing in virtually every instance in which they petition for adoption assistance after legalization of the adoption. Extenuating circumstances are most accurately characterized as the subject

of the hearing—that is, a matter to be determined at the hearing— not the grounds upon which the decision to grant or deny a hearing is made.

2. The adoptive parents assume the burden of establishing the existence of extenuating circumstances at the administrative fair hearing.

3. If the adoptive parents succeed in establishing the existence of extenuating circumstances, the next question before the hearing examiner is whether or not the child met the eligibility requirements for Title IV-E adoption assistance.

4. The state or agency is responsible for making eligibility determinations. If the state has determined that the adoptive child does not meet the eligibility requirements for Title IV-E adoption assistance, it is responsible for presenting evidence to support its determination at the hearing. If the evidence regarding the child's eligibility is not available at the time of the hearing, the hearing examiner may order the agency to determine eligibility as part of the hearing decision.

5. The adoptive parents share the burden of proof in that they must be prepared to respond with evidence of their own to a determination by the state that the child does not meet one or more of the eligibility requirements for Title IV-E adoption assistance. This responsibility, however, presupposes that an eligibility determination has been made. If there is no record that an eligibility determination has been made, the adoptive parents must cooperate in presenting information about the child's special needs, but they do not assume the entire burden of establishing the child's eligibility.

Should the adoptive family be prepared to present information pertaining to the child's eligibility for Title IV-E adoption assistance at the administrative fair hearing?

As part of their federal due process rights, the adoptive parents must be given adequate notice in cases where the state proposes to "discontinue, terminate, suspend or reduce assistance..." [45 CFR Chapter 11 205.10 (a) (4)]. *Adequate notice*, according to federal regulations, "means a written notice that includes a statement of what action the agency intends to take, the reasons for the intended action" and "the specific regulations supporting such action...." The requirement for adequate notice of agency decisions assumes the state's responsibility for making eligibility determinations and communicating them to the applicant. These due process rights apply whether the application for adoption assistance is submitted before or after the final decree of adoption.

Because an eligibility determination or (redetermination) must be made before adoption assistance may be established, parents should thoroughly familiarize themselves with the eligibility standards and prepare as best they can to respond to any arguments put forth by the agency that the child does not meet one of the Title IV-E adoption assistance requirements. In keeping with the requirement for adequate notice, the written response to the adoptive parents' application or letter of request for adoption assistance after legalization should provide some guidance to the issues that will arise at the hearing. For example, if the agency denies the child's eligibility for reasons other than the fact that the adoption was legalized without provision for adoption assistance, the parents should come to the hearing prepared to respond to those reasons.

Until all states have well-established guidelines for dealing with appeals for adoption assistance after legalization, however, applicants should not take it for granted that they will always be fully informed in advance of the hearing about the issues that will be addressed. Adoptive parents pursuing the first wave of appeals in a given state may encounter hearing examiners and agency representatives who have little or no experience with federal policy changes affecting Title IV-E adoption assistance policy.

If confronted by eligibility questions for the first time in an administrative fair hearing, parents should certainly point out their right to adequate notice and demand that sufficient time be allotted to settle the issue at hand. Given the inconsistencies that adoptive parents are bound to encounter, however, it makes good sense for them to learn as much as possible about potential controversy regarding their child's eligibility. Agencies are often quite willing to discuss their views as to whether they believe the child meets the eligibility requirements for adoption assistance prior to the hearing. Parents should feel free to contact the agency in order to obtain as clear a picture as possible regarding eligibility issues that they may need to address.

Below are several scenarios that might occur at the initial administrative fair hearing:

Scenario 1: The agency denies adoption assistance on the grounds that the adoption has been legalized and that the child did not meet the AFDC relatedness requirement because there was no record that the biological mother had received AFDC payments on the child's behalf. At the hearing, the adoptive parents first establish that extenuating circumstances existed. They then present information to show that the biological mother was in a shelter for the homeless and that the child would have been entitled to AFDC benefits at the time of removal from the mother's care and placement in a family foster home. The hearing examiner finds the evidence of the adoptive parents persuasive, declares the child eligible for adoption assistance, and orders the agency to proceed with the negotiation of an adoption assistance agreement.

Scenario 2: The agency denies adoption assistance on the grounds that the adoption has been legalized. At the hearing, the adoptive parents succeed in establishing that extenuating circumstances existed, but there is insufficient information as to whether the child met the eligibility requirements for adoption assistance. The adoptive parents contend that federal due process requires that they be given adequate notice of any eligibility issues that will be addressed at the hearing and that the agency—not the parents—is responsible for making eligibility determinations. The hearing examiner finds this argument persuasive and orders the agency to redetermine eligibility for adoption assistance as if the adoption had not been legalized. The hearing examiner also orders that if the child is found eligible, the agency should proceed to negotiate an adoption assistance agreement as if the adoption had not been legalized. The agency is required to report its findings back to the hearing examiner within 30 days. The agency subsequently determines that the child is eligible. (If the agency denies eligibility, the parents may request another hearing.)

Scenario 3: The hearing establishes that extenuating circumstances existed *and* the agency stipulates that all of the remaining eligibility requirements were met. The hearing examiner declares the child eligible for Title IV-E adoption assistance and orders the agency to negotiate an adoption assistance agreement.

Scenario 4: The agency denies the family's request for adoption assistance on the grounds that the adoption has been finalized and the family requests an administrative fair hearing. From their informal discussions with the agency, the adoptive parents anticipate that the AFDC relatedness requirement may become an issue during the hearing. They acquire information to show that the child would have been entitled to AFDC benefits at the time of removal from the biological mother's home and placement in out-of-home care had an application been made, as the biological mother had lost her job due to drug dependency and had little or no income. The hearing examiner rejects the adoptive parents' argument. The adoptive parents respond that they were not given adequate prior notice of the issues that would be considered at the hearing as required by federal law and request another hearing to address any eligibility requirements that may be at issue. Failing to obtain this, the adoptive parents appeal the hearing decision.

Establishing Adoption Assistance Payments

Once the child's eligibility for adoption assistance has been determined following an administrative fair hearing, when may adoption assistance payments begin?

Federal law states that adoption assistance payments are established by written agreement between the adoptive parents and the state or agency based on a consideration of the child's needs and the family's circumstances. After the hearing process has established the child's eligibility for adoption assistance, negotiations for an adoption assistance payment should proceed as if the adoption had not yet been legalized. Once the amount is established in a written agreement, payments may begin.

Is an actual discussion and negotiation with adoptive parents a required part of the process for determining the amount of adoption assistance and signing an agreement?

Yes. Adoption assistance is different than federal public assistance programs. If an agency merely tells a family what it may receive on behalf of the adoptive child—with no opportunity for a discussion of the child's needs and family's circumstances— it is not in full compliance with federal law.

In the years following the enactment of the original Title IV-E adoption assistance legislation, federal officials have made it clear that an adoption assistance agreement should follow a thorough discussion of the adoptive child's needs and the circumstances of the adoptive family. PIQ 90-02 actually employs the term *negotiation* in discussing how the amount of adoption assistance should be determined. Applicable sections of federal law, it states, allow for "circumstances of the adopting parents to be taken into consideration, in conjunction with the needs of the child, in determining the amount of adoption assistance. In doing so, the [s]tate should consider what it would take to incorporate a specific child, with his or her specific needs, into a particular household." The policy interpretation goes on to say that "families with the same income and similar circumstances will not necessarily agree on identical types or amounts of assistance. The uniqueness of each child/family situation may result in different amounts of payment. Consistency is not the goal."

Federal policy urges that adoptive parents and agency professionals sit down and formulate a postadoption plan of support based on a mutual consideration of the child's background, the child's future needs, and the family's situation. The specific terms of that plan of support are to be reflected in the adoption assistance agreement.

In reality, however, tight budgets place limitations on the adoptive parent's ability to negotiate adoption assistance payment rates. Most states employ payment rate ceilings based on a child's age, the foster care payment rates, the severity of a child's special needs or some combination of these factors. These rate ceilings have the practical effect of establishing boundaries on the amount of postadoptive support to which a state will commit.

Current federal policy does not address the problem of how a dollar amount of adoption assistance that is consistent with the child's needs can be negotiated in states where payment rates are inadequate. Recent policy interpretations take a step toward the empowerment of adoptive parents, however, by requiring that agencies treat parents as competent adults and engage them in a dialogue about the child's future as part of the normal process leading to the completion of an adoption assistance agreement. An adoptive parent also may appeal any agency decision that affects the amount of the adoption assistance payment by requesting an administrative fair hearing.

Does the opportunity for appeal after a final decree of adoption apply to the program for reimbursement of nonrecurring adoption expenses as well as to ongoing adoption assistance?
Although PIQ 92-02 does not specifically refer to it, the appeal procedures and guidelines set forth in the policy statement would appear to apply to the program for the reimbursement of nonrecurring adoption expenses as well as to Title IV-E adop-

tion assistance. The program provides reimbursement of up to $2,000 per child for adoption related expenses such as:

- Adoptive home study;
- Legal fees and court costs;
- Transportation, meals, and lodging;
- Reasonable adoption fees;
- Medical exams for the adoptive parents; and
- Expenses related to supervision of the adoptive placement.

Private Agency Adoptions

Are children adopted through private agencies eligible for adoption assistance after a final decree of adoption on the same terms as children who were under the care of the state prior to legalization of their adoption?

Yes. Federal PIQ 87–05 makes it clear that children who are placed for adoption by private nonprofit agencies are potentially eligible for Title IV-E adoption assistance. "The Title IV-E agency," notes the PIQ, "may not exclude them from consideration or approval, if they are otherwise eligible for adoption assistance...." The procedures and criteria for obtaining adoption assistance after a final decree of adoption apply to children placed by private agencies licensed in their respective states, as well as to those who were in the care of the state prior to legalization.

Intercountry and Nonagency Adoptions *

Are intercountry and nonagency adoptions eligible for Title IV-E adoption assistance after the final decree of adoption?

---

* Although Title IV-E adoption assistance focuses on agency adoptions, state regulations vary. Parents adopting special-needs children should not automatically assume that all children adopted without the involvement of an agency are ineligible for the program. SSI-eligible children, for example, may meet adoption assistance eligibility requirements in both

Historically, children adopted internationally and those placed for adoption without the involvement of a public or private agency have had limited access to Title IV-E adoption assistance. A major obstacle to eligibility for children of intercountry adoptions has been the lack of an established method for determining if they meet the AFDC relatedness standard. In addition, a number of states specifically limited adoption assistance to children who were in the care of public or private agencies at the time of adoptive placement.

SSI eligibility appears to represent one potential avenue of access to Title IV-E adoption assistance for intercountry and nonagency adoptions. SSI disability criteria are now easier for children to meet as the result of a 1990 U.S. Supreme Court Decision, *Zebley v. U.S. Department of Health and Human Services*. (See appendix B for information about the Zebley Implementation Hotline.)

For SSI to be an effective vehicle for the establishment of Title IV-E adoption assistance, a successful argument would have to be made that:

1. The child's current special needs meets SSI disability standards and the disability existed prior to legalization of the adoption; and

2. Income to the child prior to legalization of the adoption did not exceed SSI income eligibility standards.

Adoption agencies and families often face a procedural hurdle in attempting after legalization of the adoption to reconstruct a child's eligibility for SSI. Unlike adoption assistance, SSI employs a means test and examines income *before* moving on to a consideration of the child's disability. Prior to legalization of the adoption, the income of the person or persons

---

domestic and intercountry adoptions, whether or not an agency is involved. Some individual states may also make other exceptions for special-needs children adopted without benefit of an agency. International and domestic nonagency adoptions are also potentially eligible for federally funded reimbursement of nonrecurring adoption expenses.

adopting the child is not counted in SSI eligibility determinations because they are not yet the legal parents. The eligibility process usually proceeds to a consideration of the child's disability because the child rarely has income of his or her own.

After legalization of the adoption, however, obtaining a disability determination becomes more difficult. In most cases, the adoptive family's income will exceed SSI guidelines. If a child is ruled ineligible because the adoptive parents' income is too high, the eligibility process is halted.

Applicants would appear to have two options available to them when faced with this procedural obstacle to obtaining a disability determination.

1. Appeal the case to a higher level supervisor in the Social Security Administration, explaining that the purpose of the disability determination is to secure federal adoption assistance for the child. Some adoptive parents report success with this "don't take no for an answer" approach.

2. Obtain a list of SSI disability categories, then try to document the child's current disability from doctors' or other practitioners' statements and make a case that the disability is such that it existed prior to the adoption. Down syndrome, cerebral palsy, and attention deficit hyperactivity disorder are examples of SSI disabilities.

   Example: A family in Virginia who had legalized an intercountry adoption some years before was awarded Title IV-E adoption assistance after basing their administrative fair hearing appeal on the contention that their child met the requirements for SSI prior to the adoption. It is important to reiterate that in addition to the disability criteria, a successful appeal would require the child to have meet the income guidelines prior to legalization. In cases where the parents' income currently exceeds SSI standards, it must be successfully argued that only the child's income counted prior to legalization because the child was not yet the legal responsibility of the adoptive family.

It is too early to know if SSI eligibility will become an effective means of obtaining adoption assistance for other families involved in intercountry or nonagency adoptions. Questions about the eligibility of adoptees from such adoptions have arisen as federal policy interpretations have increased access to the adoption assistance program. Adoptive parents facing expensive medical or mental health services have little to lose by pursuing appeals for adoption assistance in such cases. If nothing else, administrative fair hearing decisions should help to clarify elements of uncertainty in the program.

States, of course, are understandably anxious about any policy change that will significantly increase program costs. Only a limited number of children adopted from other countries will meet SSI standards, however, and relatively few of the infants adopted without the involvement of agencies will qualify. For those children who may qualify for Title IV-E adoption assistance through SSI, the policy debate generated by administrative fair hearings will allow states to consider the cost effectiveness of federal adoption assistance as a means of aiding adoptive families who are under emotional and financial stress.

Where do families who adopted a child from abroad or adopted without agency involvement apply if they wish to pursue an appeal for adoption assistance after legalization?

Because of limited participation in the program, procedures for appeal are even more uncertain in the case of nonagency and intercountry adoptions than in those instances in which the child was in the care of a public or private agency at the time of adoptive placement. Parents involved in nonagency adoptions should contact the adoption section at the state department of human services located in the state where the final decree of adoption was issued. The family will probably go through the same public agency that they would have gone to for adoption assistance had the application been submitted prior to legalization.

In the case of agency adoptions, whether domestic or intercountry, appeals should be made through the administrative fair hearing system in the state where the public or private agency that held guardianship of the child at the time of adoptive placement is located. The adoptive family should contact the adoption unit at the state department of human services for information about how to proceed.

PART 2
Retroactive Adoption Assistance Payments

Obtaining Retroactive Payments

Are adoptive families eligible for retroactive adoption assistance payments?

PIQ 92-02 indicates that states may make retroactive payments to adoptive families whose children become eligible for adoption assistance after legalization as the result of a fair hearing decision. States that agree to make retroactive payments may then claim reimbursement for the federal portion of the payment. That reimbursement is always at least 50% and may run as high as 80% of the cost.

What is the basic justification for retroactive payments?

The establishment of adoption assistance after legalization is based on the finding that the child would have been determined eligible for adoption assistance except for a lack of information or some sort of error or omission. The argument that the child *should have been* determined to be eligible for adoption assistance prior to legalization leads to the conclusion that the child *would have been* receiving adoption assistance benefits since that time.

May the adoptive parents pursue a retroactive payment that is greater than the amount that is eligible for federal reimbursement?

There are no specified limits on the amount of the retroactive payment that an adoptive parent may pursue. States, of course, could be expected to be more resistant to retroactive payments for which there is no reimbursement.

May an adoptive parent request a hearing to determine the child's eligibility and request retroactive adoption assistance payments at the same time?

Yes, in making a written request for a hearing to determine the child's eligibility for adoption assistance, an adoptive parent might also include the issue of retroactive benefits in the hearing request by adding: "If my child is found eligible for the adoption assistance program, I also request that retroactive adoption assistance payments be awarded from the date of the final decree of adoption [or date of adoptive placement]." Such a request should ensure that the adoptive parent will not have to go through a separate hearing process to consider retroactive payments if the child is found eligible for adoption assistance. If the adoptive parent includes retroactive payments as part of the original hearing request, the hearing examiner must address the issue of retroactive payments in rendering a decision.

Although a separate hearing is not required, failure to include a request for retroactive payments in the initial appeal does not foreclose future options. The family of a child who is determined to be eligible for adoption assistance may pursue retroactive payments as a separate appeals initiative if the issue was not addressed in the initial round of hearings.

Limits on Retroactive Payments

How far back may the state go in calculating retroactive adoption assistance payments and still claim federal reimbursement?

Federal law was amended in 1986 to allow adoption assistance payments to begin as early as the date of adoptive placement. When the adoptive placement was made *on or after* October 1, 1986, retroactive payments back to the date of adoptive placement are potentially eligible for federal reimbursement. The date of the interlocutory or final decree of adoption is the earliest eligibility date for retroactive payments in cases where an interlocutory or final decree of adoption was issued *before* October 1, 1986.

Are there any other limits on the amount of retroactive payment that is eligible for federal reimbursement besides the time frames?

As a matter of federal law, current adoption assistance payments are only eligible for federal reimbursement up to an amount that equals the level of support the child would receive if the child were in a family foster home appropriate to the child's age and special needs. Presumably then, the maximum retroactive payment that would be eligible for federal reimbursement would be one that is equal to the family foster care payment that the child would have received during the period in question.

If a state's adoption assistance payment rates were lower than the foster care rates during the period in question, then presumably federal reimbursement would only be available up to the adoption assistance rates that were in effect at the time.

> **Example:** If the family foster care rate for the child would have been $400 per month, but state regulations limited the adoption assistance payments to $300 per month, $300 is the maximum retroactive payment that would be eligible for federal reimbursement.

Are any states making retroactive adoption assistance payments?

In December 1993, Ohio put a rule into effect that awards retroactive adoption assistance payments on a regular basis after an administrative fair hearing establishes the child's eligibility for future payments. Other states are in various stages of grappling with this issue.

Retroactive Medicaid Payments

Did PIQ 92-02 address the issue of retroactive Medicaid benefits in cases where adoptive families have incurred huge medical bills?

No, PIQ 92-02 only addressed the issue of adoption assistance payments. In issuing PIQ 92-02, the federal Children's Bureau probably felt that it had no authority to deal with the issue of retroactive Medicaid benefits because federal Medicaid policy is under the purview of another branch of the U.S. Department of Health and Human Services, the Health Care Financing Administration.

Medicaid applicants and recipients have separate administrative fair hearing rights under federal law. Adoptive families could presumably petition for retroactive Medicaid benefits through the state's fair hearing process. A request for retroactive Medicaid benefits could either be pursued as part of the original appeal for adoption assistance eligibility or as a separate hearing issue after the child was determined to be eligible for adoption assistance.

PART 3
Appealing the Administrative Hearing Decision

What steps may adoptive parents take if the initial administrative fair hearing results in a denial of the child's eligibility for adoption assistance or of the request for retroactive adoption assistance payments?

Although terminology may differ from state to state, the basic steps in the fair hearing process are the same.

The decision of the hearing officer must be communicated to the adoptive parents in writing. If the initial hearing decision goes against the adoptive parents, the notification letter must also provide information about the next level of appeal.

This next level in a number of states is an *administrative review* of the hearing, usually by a section in the state's department of human services. The administrative review is not another hearing, but a reconsideration of the hearing decision based on the hearing record and relevant state regulations. The decision arising from this administrative review must also be communicated to the adoptive parent in writing, along with information about the next level of appeal. In states where there is no interim step or administrative review of administrative hearing decisions, the next level of appeal is a local court.

An appeal to a local court for a *judicial review* of the administrative hearing decision is the final step in the hearing process. The court review is not a hearing but a reconsideration of the arguments for adoption assistance eligibility, retroactive payments, the amount of adoption assistance, or some other issue presented in the first two steps of the appeals process.

Because the administrative review and judicial review stages of the appeals process are not hearings, it is crucial that the adoptive parents present all the essential arguments and documentation at the original hearing so that they become part of the record that is reviewed. Agency decisions concerning the child's eligibility for adoption assistance and hearing decisions should contain information about time limits for appeal as well as the next step in the hearing process. Parents should be careful to observe filing deadlines.

Is it practical for an adoptive parent to pursue an appeal beyond the initial hearing decision?

The adoptive family has virtually nothing to lose by appealing an initial hearing decision to the next level. Before proceeding with a petition for judicial review, however, it might be advisable for the adoptive parents to consult with an adoptive parent support group or advocacy organization to get a clearer sense of the benefits of appealing and the potential costs in time and dollars.

While there is no cost for participating in the first two steps of the hearing process, petitioning for a judicial review generally involves modest filing fees. In addition, adoptive parents who have not enlisted legal counsel to represent them in the first two phases of the hearing process often hire an attorney at the judicial review phase to file the necessary papers and to represent them before the court.

The following observations may be useful to parents who are considering whether to file for judicial review. They are based on the practical experiences of adoptive families with administrative fair hearings in recent years.

1. Fair hearing and administrative review decisions are usually based upon existing state regulations. If there are no state regulations or policy guidelines to cover the existing situation, the appeal is usually denied. In practical terms, this means that adoptive parents who are challenging an existing state policy or raising an issue that is not yet covered in state regulations or guidelines may be denied at both the initial hearing and administrative appeal stages of the appeals process.

Although there are no guarantees that the court will look beyond the existing regulations (or lack of regulations) to the larger purposes of the program, a family often must be willing to push the appeal to the judicial review stage before the case has a chance of being considered on its merits. Judicial review decisions in favor of adoptive families played a significant role in bringing about the policy change that opened up access to adoption assistance after legalization, the policy revision reflected in PIQ 92-02.

2. State agencies do not like to let courts decide issues because courts are unpredictable. Once an adoptive parent has filed for judicial review, the state agency must decide whether to address the substance of the case or let a court make the decision. To avoid a court decision, the agency may offer to negotiate a settlement with the adoptive parents. In Ohio, the settlement of several appeals on a case-by-case basis eventually created a demand for a change in state policy, first on the question of eligibility for adoption assistance after legalization, and later on the issue of retroactive adoption assistance payments.

An offer by the state agency to discuss a settlement means that the child's and the family's individual circumstances will be addressed, not just current state policy. The possibility of negotiating a settlement as an alternative to a court decision is another reason why an adoptive parent should consider hiring an attorney to file for the judicial review.

PART 4
Summary

Although specific procedures for filing an appeal for adoption assistance after legalization may differ from state to state, they are likely to follow a pattern somewhat like the following:

1. The adoptive family contacts the adoption section of the state's department of human services and obtains information on how to petition for Title IV-E adoption assistance after a final decree of adoption.

2. The adoptive family completes an application form or a written statement requesting adoption assistance and submits it to the appropriate public agency.

3. The agency denies eligibility for adoption assistance, usually on the basis of timeliness—that is, because the adoption has been legalized. The agency may also determine that the child does not meet one of the other eligibility requirements for Title IV-E adoption assistance. In addition to the reasons for denying eligibility, the agency's written response contains notification of the right of appeal and information about how to request an administrative fair hearing.

4. The adoptive family requests an administrative fair hearing and one is scheduled. If the adoptive family has decided to pursue retroactive payments in addition to eligibility for future benefits, it includes a request for retroactive payments in the petition for a hearing.

5. At the hearing, the adoptive family attempts to establish that extenuating circumstances existed and prevented the family from applying for, or the child from receiving, adoption assistance prior to the final decree of adoption.

6. If necessary, the adoptive family makes a case for the child's eligibility, particularly if the agency intends to argue that, in addition to filing for adoption assistance after finalization, the child did not meet one of the other

basic requirements for Title IV-E adoption assistance.

7a. The hearing examiner establishes that extenuating circumstances existed, and orders that eligibility for adoption assistance be determined without regard to the normal timeliness standard; or alternatively, the hearing examiner establishes that extenuating circumstances existed *and* that all of the remaining eligibility requirements were met. The hearing examiner declares the child eligible for Title IV-E adoption assistance and orders the agency to negotiate an adoption assistance agreement (go to 8a) *or*

7b. The hearing examiner determines that extenuating circumstances were not present, the child did not meet one of the eligibility requirements for Title IV-E adoption assistance, or the child is eligible for adoption assistance but not eligible for retroactive payments. The decision is communicated in writing and contains information about the next step in the appeals process (go to 8b or 8c).

8a. The child's eligibility is established as a result of the hearing process. The adoptive family negotiates an adoption assistance agreement with the agency as if the adoption had not been finalized; or

8b. The adoptive family appeals the hearing decision that the child was not eligible for IV-E adoption assistance by filing for an administrative review by the state's department of human services. (In some states, the next level of appeal would be a judicial review by the local court.)

8c. The child's eligibility is established as a result of the administrative fair hearing process, but the hearing denies the request for retroactive payments. The family negotiates an adoption assistance agreement for future benefits, but appeals the denial of retroactive payments by requesting an administrative review by the state's department of human services. (In some states, the next level of appeal would be a judicial review by the local court.)

9. The parent loses the appeal at the administrative review and decides to file for a judicial review. The administrative review decision contains information about how to file for a judicial review.

10. The state offers to negotiate a settlement in place of a court decision or the state lets the judicial review decide the appeal.

3 Costs and Benefits of Retroactive Adoption Assistance Payments

States are understandably reluctant to address the issue of retroactive adoption assistance payments because of the unknown costs involved. Ohio's experience with retroactive payments, however, suggests that the states' burden for retroactive adoption assistance payments may be partially offset by a number of mitigating factors.

1. **Payments are eligible for federal reimbursement.** The federal share of adoption assistance payments is the same as the federal share of the state's Medicaid payments. From 50% to 80% of the cost of retroactive adoption assistance payments may be eligible for federal reimbursement.

2. **Retroactive payments may take pressure off of the state's postadoption services budgets.** Candidates for retroactive adoption assistance payments are often experiencing the same types of problems as families that come to the state for help with postadoptive medical or mental health services for their children. Postadoption services programs are usually funded entirely with state money and fall far short of meeting existing levels of need. Retroactive adoption assistance payments provide a means of accessing additional federal dollars to supplement underfunded postadoption support services.

3. **The appeals process spreads out the costs.** The requirement that each adoptive family must establish the child's eligibility through the state's administrative fair hearing process

has the effect of spreading out claims for retroactive payments. The hearing process often takes weeks or months to complete. States, therefore, can only handle so many retroactive payment appeals during the course of a year.

4. **Claims for retroactive payments will decrease in a few years.** The appeals process to establish adoption assistance after legalization is a measure designed to bring relief to families who adopted at a time when important information about the child's background was often not provided and special needs were often underestimated. Adoption practice has improved in recent years and information about adoption assistance is likely to be available to prospective adoptive parents. Claims for retroactive payments will increase for a few years and then will decline because the number of appeals stemming from recent adoptions will lessen due to improved access to adoption assistance programs.

5. **Retroactive payments provide a possible alternative to out-of-home care funded at state expense.** When an adoptive family's health insurance and personal resources are exhausted and the parents can no longer pay the cost of the child's medical care or therapy, the child may be placed in the care of the state to ensure that services continue to be provided. In such cases, the child usually is not eligible for Title IV-E foster care assistance because most adoptive families are not eligible for AFDC benefits. The state, therefore, must pick up the entire cost of care, except for the small portion that the adoptive family might contribute as child support. It is worth exploring federally reimbursable retroactive adoption assistance payments as at least a partial alternative to state funded care, especially if such assistance helps keep the child at home.

Ohio: A Case Study

Ohio's Department of Human Services settled 11 individual cases before the December 1993, rule on awarding retroactive adoption assistance payments went into effect. The settlements typically awarded payments back to the date of the final decree of adoption. The December rule awarded retroactive payments to most families whose children became eligible for adoption assistance after legalization as the result of an administrative fair hearing. The rule allowed payments back to the date of the final decree of adoption in the case of adoptions legalized prior to September 1988, and permitted payments back to the date of the adoption petition in the case of adoptions legalized after September 1988.

Both the individual settlements and the subsequent rule resulted in the awarding of retroactive payments on the basis of what the child would have received during the period in question, based on agency policy at the time. The retroactive payments, however, could not exceed the level of financial support that the child would have received had he or she been in family foster care instead of an adoptive home—the maximum amount that was eligible for federal reimbursement. In Ohio, as in most states, actual adoption assistance payments almost never exceed the amount eligible for federal reimbursement.

For a number of years, the maximum adoption assistance payment eligible for federal reimbursement under Ohio regulations was $250 per month. Not surprisingly, $250 was also the standard payment in most Ohio counties during those years. A typical retroactive adoption assistance payment for the same period, therefore, would also be $250 per month, going back to the date of legalization.

> **Example:** The adoption was finalized in December 1986. As a result of the fair hearing process, the child was determined to be eligible for adoption assistance in April 1994. An adoption assistance agreement for future payments was completed in May of 1994. After consulting state policy, it was determined that the child would have received $250 per month during the period in question. The retroactive adoption assistance payment was the total of $250 per month from the date of legalization to the date the adoption assistance agreement was completed.

The average retroactive adoption assistance payment awarded in the 11 settlement cases and in the first 10 cases handled in accordance with the December 1993, rule was $19,345. All but two of these 21 cases were eligible for federal reimbursement at a rate of approximately 60%. The average amount of the payment that was eligible for federal reimbursement in these 21 cases was approximately $11,607, leaving about $7,738 per case as the sole responsibility of the state.

Overall, $406,253 in retroactive payments were awarded for the 21 cases. The federal share of the payments came to about $243,741 and the state's share amounted to approximately $162,494.

A review of administrative fair hearings decisions issued from January through June 1994, suggests that as many as 32 cases may result in some form of retroactive benefits being issued, with an average payment of over $20,000 per case. Projecting six eligible cases per month for the remainder of the year, retroactive payments for 68 cases in calendar year 1994 would total around $1.4 million. Assuming that a portion of the cases would not be eligible for federal reimbursement because of past state regulations affecting private agencies, the estimated federal share of the retroactive payments would come to over $700,000. The projected cost to the state would be about $600,000.

Other states might face higher retroactive payments per case because Ohio's adoption assistance payment rates have been comparatively low for a number of years. On the other hand, Ohio, with its large population and liberal regulations for awarding retroactive payments, might be expected to have a higher volume of cases than most other states.

A Concluding Note

As states contemplate the policy implications of retroactive adoption assistance benefits, it is worth considering once again the advantages of investing in adoption over the various forms of out-of-home care. Westat's 1993 "Study of Adoption Assistance, Impact and Outcomes," conducted for the U.S. Department of Health and Human Services, found that adoption assistance "clearly represents a substantial savings over continued foster care." The Westat report estimated that "federal and state governments will save a total of approximately $1.6 billion in connection with the group of 40,700 children adopted with assistance during the 1983 to 1987 period." Moreover, "this estimated savings considers only the difference in administrative costs between foster care and adoption assistance up to the time the children reach age 18 and would normally be discharged from foster care." The Westat study also found that children in out-of-home care were more likely to experience emotional problems, have problems with the law, and need public assistance, and less likely to hold a job and complete high school than adopted children. Each of these outcomes represents economic as well as social costs.

4   ADOPTIVE FAMILIES AND THE SYSTEM

Changing Attitudes Toward Adoption Assistance

Attitudes toward adoption assistance have changed markedly in recent years. Where once it was common for agencies to introduce the subject of adoption subsidy only as a last resort, today, growing numbers (perhaps a majority) of adoption professionals view exploration of adoption assistance benefits as an integral part of the adoption process itself.

Information and Power

Parents who adopt special-needs children often discover the need for assertiveness and persistence as they confront a fragmented and underfunded social service system. For such parents, information is indeed the first step to empowerment. Adoptive parents have benefited greatly from increased information about adoption subsidy programs provided by state and local agencies and a growing network of adoptive family support groups. Lack of factual information, however, is not the only inhibiting factor where adoption assistance is concerned. Adoptive parents have traditionally faced a variety of cultural and institutional obstacles as well.

Cultural Obstacles

Prospective mothers and fathers, particularly those adopting for the first time, are understandably preoccupied with the excitement and responsibilities of impending parenthood. In those anxious days preceding an adoption, parents who would have no hesitation in shopping for the best health care plan for their growing family often report feeling uncomfortable about the issue of adoption subsidy. This uneasiness is born of a fierce desire to make the child their own and is reinforced by a number of cultural clichés—often unspoken, but clearly communicating the same essential message—such as:

- "People should not be paid to adopt a child!"
- "Nobody helped me when my biological child had problems!"
- "When you adopt, you should expect to be responsible for the child."

Purveyors of such carelessly delivered messages do not pause to think how preoccupied with questions of responsibility and "entitlement" most adoptive parents must be. Adoptive parents face all the familiar challenges involved in building a family, yet often experience few of the comforting cultural rituals surrounding the actual birth of a child.

The fact that adopted children are at greater risk of experiencing medical and emotional problems than biological children substantially weakens the erroneous association of adoption subsidy with parental greed. Today, questions about the motives of the adoptive parents are more likely to arise when parents attempt to negotiate an amount of adoption assistance that is above the normal allocation or when they approach the agency for help after the adoption is legalized.

Institutional Obstacles

Federal officials now emphasize dialogue between the agency and parents aimed at tailoring adoption assistance to meet the individual circumstances of the child and family. This model, however, is still unfamiliar to many public agencies with a tradition of standard eligibility requirements and benefit packages. Moreover, while agency support for adoption subsidies has increased, confronting the gap between a child's needs and the available resources to meet those needs continues to be a frustrating experience for both agencies and families.

When parents take the position, either before or after the adoption, that the special needs of their child warrants a commitment of assistance beyond the agency's normal policy, they frequently encounter organizational structures that encourage conflict and frustration rather than negotiation. The adoption worker with whom they have been working is the agency representative most likely to be sympathetic to the family's concerns, but least likely to have authority over fiscal decisions. The administrator in charge of financial policy, on the other hand, often has an imperfect understanding of adoption issues and little direct exposure to adoptive families and their problems.

Baring one's problems to public officials is not a pleasant experience. Many families are reluctant to push for an increase in the amount of subsidy before the adoption is legalized for fear of jeopardizing the placement. Those who have already adopted often wait until the child's problems have reached a critical stage before approaching an agency for help.

Faced with budget constraints, it is not uncommon for agencies to respond to requests for additional assistance by avoiding or minimizing the parent's perception of the child's needs. Instead of acknowledging the parents' anxieties as real, the agency may unintentionally play down the severity of the problem and define the child's needs in terms of available resources. The parents' perception that the agency is denying their children's problems undermines trust. The message received by the adoptive parents is that at best, their proposal for adoption assistance is unreasonable. At worst, the agency seems to be calling their motives for adopting the child into question.

There are no easy solutions to the problems engendered by limited resources. As long as severe abuse and neglect are the common plight of substantial numbers of children waiting for adoption, and as long as the needs of these children continue to strain family resources, some level of conflict is inevitable. Funding problems will remain a fact of life in the foreseeable future, but conflict can be reduced by a policy of candor as reflected in the following practices:

1. Acknowledge the child's problems as real and recognize the adoptive parent's struggle to provide adequate services for the child.

Denial of the adoptive family's concerns or distress is a major source of conflict. Validating the adoptive family's concerns, on the other hand, signals a responsibility on the part of county and state agencies to help secure needed postadoption services and financial assistance.

2. Provide complete information about adoption assistance and subsidy programs even if the agency is not able to provide the optimum amount of support.

Another major source of anger among adoptive parents is the discovery that they have not been informed about existing subsidy programs. Adoptive parents are well aware of the struggle involved in securing effective educational or mental health services for a special needs child. They are often remarkably forbearing about rules and red tape if they are convinced that the agency is doing its best to help.

Important Points to Consider

Unless health care reform ushers in a comprehensive system of support for adopted children with special needs, advocacy will continue to be a major responsibility of their adoptive parents. While the following ideas certainly do not solve the problem of limited resources, it is hoped that they will help adoptive parents negotiate adoption assistance benefits for their children with more confidence and help adoption professionals to broaden their understanding of subsidy as an investment in families if they have not already done so.

1. Adoption subsidy is a form of health insurance.

With the current cost of medical care, the refusal to accept health insurance and the insistence on paying for all of the family's medical expenses out of pocket would not normally be regarded as a mark of parental virtue. Because catastrophic accidents or illnesses can and do occur, most people would see such a decision as needlessly placing family members at risk.

Adoption assistance and subsidy programs are in essence forms of health insurance designed to sustain a child in a new family. Negotiating an agreement for comprehensive support through an adoption subsidy should be viewed in the same light as negotiating the most comprehensive health care plan possible for one's family.

2. Adoptive families are social resources.

One of the most impressive things about adoptive parents is that while they often display an inspiring commitment to the children they incorporate into their families, they do not characteristically think of themselves as extraordinary people. Examined in a larger social context, however, adoptive families of waiting children emerge as a valuable social resource for a number of reasons:

- The primary alternative to a permanent adoptive family is some type of family foster or institutional care funded at public expense. As researcher Richard Barth has noted, out-of-home care is not only more expensive to administer, but it ends at age 18. As parents with young adult children will attest, the need for support does not end at age 18 or even 21. The presence of a caring family often determines whether a young person makes a successful transition to adulthood. A significant portion of young homeless adults are products of the out-of-home care system.

- Providing permanent homes for waiting children without families involves a substantial financial as well as emotional investment on the part of adoptive parents. Barth reminds us that providing a new family for a child through adoption is the ultimate volunteer program. In a 1993 article based on research in California, he concluded that $50,000 was a conservative estimate of the average parent's financial contribution to the child from the date of adoption to adulthood.

- Adoption results in substantial savings in the administrative costs of out-of-home care. A comprehensive "Study of Adoption Assistance, Impact and Outcomes" conducted by

Westat for the U.S. Department of Health and Human Services concluded that adoption assistance clearly "represents a substantial savings over continued foster care." The 1993 Westat report estimated that "federal and state governments will save a total of approximately $1.6 billion in connection with the group of 40,700 children adopted with assistance during the 1983 to 1987 period. This estimated savings considers only the difference in administrative costs between foster care and adoption assistance up to the time the children reach age 18 and would normally be discharged from foster care."

- If the adoptive family cannot meet the child's medical or mental health needs, the child frequently ends up in out-of-home care at state expense. Once an adoptive family's health insurance is exhausted and personal resources depleted, placing the child in the care of the state is sometimes the only means through which services can be obtained.

3. In negotiating adoption assistance, the focus should remain on the current and future needs of the child

The various adoption assistance and subsidy programs should be regarded as potential resources to be combined in a comprehensive plan of support for the child. Federal policy, as noted earlier, now assumes that the adoptive parents and the public agency will negotiate face to face. The purpose of the dialogue between the parents and agency is to develop a realistic picture of the child's needs and the resources that will be available to meet those needs. In preparation, the adoptive parents should be provided with detailed written information about existing adoption subsidies and policies.

4. Adoption assistance is not a welfare program.

Adoption assistance and subsidy programs allow parents to incorporate a waiting child into their family. Those adoptive families who make economic sacrifices for their children with special needs should not be penalized.

APPENDIX A:
FEDERAL POLICY INTERPRETATIONS

	U.S. DEPARTMENT OF HEALTH AND HUMAN SERVICES
	Administration for Children, Youth and Families

1. Log No. ACYF-PIQ-88-06	2. Issuance Date: 12/2/88
3. Originating Office: Children's Bureau	
4. Key Word: Eligibility for Title IV-E	
Adoption Assistance	

POLICY INTERPRETATION QUESTION

TO: State Agencies Administering or Supervising the Administration of Title IV-E of the Social Security Act and Indian Tribes and Indian Tribal Organizations

SUBJECT: Eligibility for Title IV-E Adoption Assistance

STATEMENT
OF PROBLEM: Region IV has asked a question on behalf of the State of Tennessee regarding the availability of adoption assistance through the Adoption Assistance Program under title IV-E of the Social Security Act. The question concerns a couple who recently adopted two children (siblings) through the Tennessee Department of Human Services who had been living with the family in foster care for about eight years prior to adoption. The parents requested adoption assistance for both children; however, Tennessee's definition of a special needs sibling group is one which includes at least three children and the two girls were not eligible on this basis. The older child was determined eligible under the title IV-E program because of her age, but the other child was too young under the State's definition of "a child with special needs."

The parents notified the agency prior to the adoption that the younger child was experiencing neck and back pain. The child was taken to several doctors for a diagnosis which would establish the child's eligibility for assistance; however, examining physicians were unable to make a diagnosis at that time and the request for assistance was denied. Later, after the adoptions of both children had been legalized, the younger child was diagnosed as having junior rheumatoid arthritis. The parents again requested adoption assistance for the child.

-2-

The State has denied the parents' request, based on the Federal regulation (45 CFR 1356.40 (b)(1)) requiring that the adoption assistance agreement be signed and in effect prior to the final decree of adoption in order to provide assistance under title IV-E.

The parents believe the denial was unfair because the child's medical condition was not properly considered, and they also claim that they were not fully informed by the agency staff as to the eligibility requirements of the adoption assistance program. Additionally, the parents expressed fear that the State agency would deny the adoptions if they did not sign the legal papers when requested.

LEGAL AND RELATED REFERENCES:

Social Security Act, Sections 473(a) and (c) and 471(a)(12); 45 CFR 1356.40 (b)(1).

QUESTION: If the adoptive parents are able to prove to the State agency's satisfaction that all facts relevant to their request for adoption assistance were not presented at the time adoption assistance was discussed, may the State reverse an earlier decision to deny benefits under title IV-E?

ANSWER: Yes, under certain specified conditions. According to the Federal regulations at 45 CFR 1356.40(b)(1), the adoption assistance agreement must be signed and in effect at the time of or prior to the final decree of adoption in order to provide assistance under title IV-E.

However, if there are extenuating circumstances, the adoptive parents may request a fair hearing under section 471(a)(12) of the Act. If the hearing determines that all of the facts relevant to the child's eligibility were not presented at the time of the request for assistance, the State may reverse the earlier decision to deny benefits under title IV-E.

Dodje Truman Borup
COMMISSIONER

Appendices

human
development
services

U.S. DEPARTMENT OF HEALTH AND HUMAN SERVICES		
Administration for Children, Youth and Families		
1. Log No. ACYF-PIQ-90-02		**2. Issuance Date:** 10-02-90
3. Originating Office: Children's Bureau		
4. Key Word: Title IV-E		**5.** Adoption Assistance
6. Means Test		

POLICY INTERPRETATION QUESTION

TO   : State Agencies Administering or Supervising
              Administration of Title IV-E of the Social Security
              Act, Indian Tribes and Indian Tribal Organizations
              (ITOs)

SUBJECT : Title IV-E Adoption Assistance Agreements and the Use
            of a Means Test

STATEMENT OF PROBLEM:

Public Law (P.L.) 96-272, the Adoption Assistance and
Child Welfare Act of 1980, established a program of
adoption assistance for "children with special needs."
This landmark legislation was intended to provide, for
the first time, Federal financial participation with
States in a program of incentives and supports to
families adopting certain children who, because of a
variety of specific factors or conditions, could not be
adopted without assistance.

The legislative history of P.L. 96-272 indicates that
Congress at first considered the inclusion of a "means
test" as a requirement under the title IV-E adoption
assistance program. At one point in Committee
discussion, a family would not have been eligible to
receive adoption assistance if its income exceeded 150%
of the State median income for a family of four.
However, this restriction was later dropped after the
Committee noted that "we should not design a program to
foster adoptions only in those families with the least
financial capacity to care for these special needs
children." (See Congressional Record -- Senate --
S11704, August 3, 1979.)

-2-

In the years since the enactment of P.L. 96-272, States have developed their title IV-E adoption assistance programs to comply with the State Plan requirements in section 471 and the program requirements in section 473 of the Social Security Act (the Act). Recently, however, questions have been raised by a number of States, through the Regional Offices of the Office of Human Development Services, indicating that there is still uncertainty about the use of a means test and the appropriate method for negotiating an adoption assistance agreement with potential adoptive parents in relation to a child who is eligible for assistance under title IV-E.

BACKGROUND: In order to be eligible for ongoing adoption assistance payments under title IV-E, a child must be eligible for Aid to Families With Dependent Children, title IV-E Foster Care, or Supplemental Security Income for the Blind and Disabled and meet the definition of a child with special needs according to section 473(c) of the Act. Under that section, the State title IV-E agency makes a determination as to whether a child is a child with special needs, according to the following factors: the child cannot or should not be returned to the home of the parents; there exists a specific factor or condition (such as the child's age, ethnic background, emotional, physical or mental handicap, or membership in a minority or sibling group) because of which it is reasonable to conclude that the child cannot be placed for adoption without providing adoption assistance; and, except where it would be against the best interests of the child, a reasonable, but unsuccessful, effort has been made to place the child without adoption assistance.

The title IV-E regulations at 45 CFR 1356.40(c) prohibit the use of a means test in the process of selecting suitable adoptive parents for a special needs child and in negotiating an adoption assistance agreement (including the amount of the adoption assistance payment). This means that, once a child is found eligible under section 473(c) of the Act, the child's adoptive parents may not be rejected for adoption assistance or have payments reduced without their agreement because of the level of their income or other resources. The purpose of the adoption assistance program is to provide incentives for families of any economic stratum and to remove barriers to the adoption of special needs children.

3

Section 473(a)(3) of the Act states that the amount of the adoption assistance payment shall be determined through an agreement between the adoptive parents and the State or local agency and that the agreement "shall take into consideration the circumstances of the adopting parents and the needs of the child . . ." The language is interpreted to pertain to the parents' ability to incorporate the child into their household in relation to their lifestyle, standard of living and future plans and to their overall capacity to meet the immediate and future needs (including educational needs) of the child.

In some States, however, the language has been used to justify extensive investigation of the financial circumstances of the potential adoptive parents at the time of adoption and at yearly recertification periods subsequent to the adoption. There is no statutory requirement for such investigations; thus, Federal reimbursement is not available for costs associated with them.

Section 473(a)(4)(B) of the Act indicates that there are only two reasons (other than the child's age) why parents become ineligible for payments after the child is adopted: (1) the State determines that the parents are no longer legally responsible for the support of the child and (2) the State determines that the child is no longer receiving any support from the parents. The parents may also request termination of payments and services. Events not related to these conditions that occur subsequent to the adoption have no applicability to title IV-E eligibility.

LEGAL AND RELATED REFERENCES:

Section 473 of the Social Security Act; 45 CFR 1356.40(c); and ACYF-PIQ-82-02, dated January 19, 1982

INTREPRETATION TO:

Questions raised by Regional Offices regarding the development of an adoption assistance agreement and the use of a means test.

QUESTION 1: Can a State use criteria, such as State median income adjusted for family size or a sliding income scale, in determining the potential adoptive family's eligibility for adoption assistance?

RESPONSE: No. The regulations at 45 CFR 1356.40(c) prohibit the use of a means test in determining eligibility for adoption assistance payments. Therefore, States are prohibited from using criteria such as State median income or sliding income scales to determine the eligibility of adoptive parents to receive adoption assistance payments on behalf of a special needs child.

QUESTION 2: Should State policy describe the procedure used by the State to determine eligibility for and the amount of adoption assistance?

RESPONSE: Yes. The Title IV-E State Plan requires inclusion of State statutory, regulatory and policy references for each Federal statutory and regulatory requirement under title IV-E. As a result, States must address the procedures in place which meet the requirements regarding eligibility for and amount of adoption assistance as set forth in section 473 of the Act and 45 CFR 1356.40(c).

QUESTION 3: Can the State median income adjusted to family size be used as a guide to establish consistency in determining amounts of payment?

RESPONSE: No. The use of such guidelines is not appropriate to the process. During the negotiation of an adoption assistance agreement, it is important to keep in mind that the circumstances of the adopting parents and the needs of the child must be considered together. As stated in the Background section, this means the overall ability of a singular family to incorporate an individual child into the household. Families with the same incomes or in similar circumstances will not necessarily agree on identical types or amounts of assistance. The uniqueness of each child/family situation may result in different amounts of payment. Consistency is not the goal.

QUESTION 4: Some States use the family's income as one of the factors considered in determining the amount of the adoption assistance payment, since Policy Interpretation Question ACYF-PIQ-82-02, dated January 19, 1982, states: "If Mississippi uses the means test, in conjunction with the needs of the child, to determine the amount of assistance, it is a permissible tool." When determining the amount of the monthly payment, are all factors of consideration given equal weight? When setting the amount of the monthly payment, can the family's income be the major factor in determining the amount of monthly payment?

5

RESPONSE: Policy Interpretation Question ACYF-PIQ-82-02 predated
             the Final Rule, dated May 23, 1983, which takes
             precedence over previously written policy issuances.
             The regulations at 45 CFR 1356.40(c) specifically
             prohibit the use of a means test for prospective
             adoptive parents in determining their eligibility for
             payments.

             Sections 473(a)(1), (2) and (3) of the Act clearly
             indicate that eligibility for adoption assistance is
             related to the child and not the parent; therefore,
             the negotiation should focus on the needs of the
             child. As stated in the Background section, section
             473(a)(3) allows for the circumstances of the adopting
             parents to be taken into consideration, in conjunction
             with the needs of the child, in determining the amount
             of adoption assistance. In doing so, the State should
             consider what it would take to incorporate a specific
             child, with his or her specific needs, into a
             particular household.

QUESTION 5: Can the State deny an adoption assistance payment to
             potential adoptive parents who have chosen to defer
             their maximum income potential while pursuing a higher
             education? For instance, an infant is considered to
             be a special needs child because of a combination of
             medical problems and minority status. A family is
             interested in adopting but will need help with the
             medical expenses, as the child will need corrective
             surgery plus ongoing medical care. The prospective
             adoptive parents are both medical students and have
             two years to complete their internships. They request
             monthly adoption assistance payments for two years and
             ongoing medical assistance after that time. Can the
             State deny cash payments or limit assistance to
             medical care?

RESPONSE: No. The State cannot deny adoption assistance
             payments because the adoptive parents have chosen to
             defer their maximum income potential while pursuing a
             higher education. The adoptive parents' income is not
             relevant to the child's eligibility for adoption
             assistance payments. As stated in an earlier
             response, the eligibility for adoption assistance is
             related to the child and not the parent. The example
             can be used, however, to demonstrate the process
             described in response to previous questions; that is,
             that adoption assistance agreements are developed for
             individual situations. In this case, the discussion
             of payment would take into consideration the parents'
             plans and their request for assistance to meet the
             needs of the child during a specific period. This,

too, could be adjusted at some time in the future. If agreement cannot be reached between the agency and the adoptive parents, they have the right to request a fair hearing.

QUESTION 6:   In a similar situation, parents already receiving assistance payments return to school for a one-year training program and request an increase in the amount of payment for that period of time to meet the needs of the child. Can the agency deny this request based on the voluntary nature of the change in income level or the fact that the modification in income may not relate to the original need or circumstances at the time of the initial agreement?

RESPONSE: The State cannot arbitrarily reject such requests. Section 473(a)(3) requires the State to consider the circumstances of the adopting parents when determining the amount of payment and allows for periodic readjustment depending upon changes in such circumstances. The statute does not limit the changes in circumstances to those which are beyond the parents control. As in the response to Question #5 above, the agency should consider such requests in a renegotiation of the adoption assistance agreement with regard for the parents' plans for meeting the needs of the child during a specific time period. If the agency refuses to consider a renegotiation of the adoption assistance agreement, the adoptive parents have the right to request a fair hearing.

DISCUSSION: The title IV-E Adoption Assistance Program has a broad purpose and, unlike other public assistance programs in the Social Security Act, it is intended to encourage an action which will be of lifelong social benefit to a certain category of children and not generally to meet short-term monetary needs during a temporary period of economic crisis.

Under title IV-E, the term "adoption assistance" means, literally, to assist the adoption of children with special needs. Experience in public child welfare agencies has shown that, in the past, many children with special problems and disabilities have grown up in foster homes or institutions, without the security of belonging to a family of their own. Assisting in the adoption of such children is not only beneficial for the children and enriching for families, but is also cost-beneficial to State agencies in that administrative costs in the adoption assistance program can be far less than in the foster care program.

Appendices

7

Means testing concepts such as those illustrated in
the examples cited in this policy issuance are not
appropriate in the title IV-E adoption assistance
program and should not be acted upon in the
negotiation of an agreement with prospective adoptive
parents. Adoptive parents are selected for their
ability to provide permanent and stable homes for
special needs children and are not expected to change
their long-term plans because of the adoption of such
children. Under the title IV-E program, even though
adoption assistance payments are made, the agency does
not control or participate in family choices regarding
lifestyle or career plans.

Wade F. Horn, Ph.D.
Commissioner

ACF **Administration for Children and Families**	**U.S. DEPARTMENT OF HEALTH AND HUMAN SERVICES** Administration on Children, Youth and Families

1. Log No. ACF-PIO-92-02	2. Issuance Date: June 25, 1992
3. Originating Office: Children's Bureau	
4. Key Word: Fair Hearing and Extenuating Circumstances	

POLICY INTERPRETATION QUESTION

TO   : State Agencies Administering or Supervising the
               Administration of Title IV-E of the Social Security
               Act, Indian Tribes and Indian Tribal Organizations

SUBJECT   : Clarification Regarding ACYF-PIQ-88-06, Dated
               December 2, 1988, and Situations Which Would
               Constitute "Extenuating Circumstances" for the
               Purpose of a Fair Hearing for Denial of Title IV-E
               Adoption Assistance

LEGAL AND RELATED REFERENCES:

               Sections 473(a) and (c), 471(a)(12) and 1132(a) of
               the Social Security Act, 45 CFR 1356.40(b)(1),
               45 CFR 95.7, ACYF-PIQ-83-4, Dated October 26, 1983
               and ACYF-PIQ-88-06, Dated December 2, 1988

BACKGROUND:

Policy Interpretation Question, ACYF-PIQ-88-06, dated December 2,
1988, set forth conditions, after the finalization of an
adoption, under which a State may reverse an earlier decision to
deny title IV-E adoption assistance benefits. It stated that
Federal regulations at 45 CFR 1356.40(b)(1) require that the
adoption assistance agreement be signed and in effect at the time
of or prior to the final decree of adoption. However, if the
adoptive parents were denied benefits and there are extenuating
circumstances, the adoptive parents may request a fair hearing.
The policy issuance goes on to state that, if the hearing
determines that all of the facts relevant to the child's
eligibility were not presented at the time of the request for
assistance, the State may reverse the earlier decision to deny
benefits under title IV-E.

-2-

INTERPRETATION TO:

Questions raised with regard to what constitutes "extenuating circumstances" for the purpose of a fair hearing under the title IV-E adoption assistance program.

QUESTION 1:

The case situation described in ACYF-PIQ-88-06 spoke to a child's medical condition which was not properly diagnosed prior to adoption as being grounds for a fair hearing. Would a change in Federal statute, regulation or policy constitute grounds for a fair hearing as well?

RESPONSE:

No. Changes in Federal statute, regulation or policy normally are effective only prospectively. Since the previous statute, regulation or policy is in effect until such a change is made, a change would not constitute grounds for a fair hearing.

QUESTION 2:

With respect to the State agency's responsibilities in the administration of the program, some concern has been expressed over the seeming paradox between notifying and advising prospective adoptive parents of the adoption assistance program and making a reasonable, but unsuccessful, effort to place a child without adoption assistance as required by section 473(c)(2)(B) of the Social Security Act. Please clarify this issue.

RESPONSE:

In an effort to find an adoptive home for a child, the agency should first look at a number of families in order to locate the most suitable family for the child. Once the agency has determined that placement with a certain family would be the most suitable for the child, then full disclosure should be made of the child's background, as well as known and potential problems. If the child meets the State's definition of special needs with regard to specific factors or conditions, then the agency can pose the question of whether the prospective adoptive parents are willing to adopt without a subsidy. If they say that they cannot adopt the child without a subsidy, the agency would meet the requirement in 473(c)(2)(B) that there be a reasonable, but unsuccessful, effort to place the child without providing adoption assistance.

It was the intent of Congress, with the establishment of the adoption assistance program, to increase significantly the number of children placed in permanent homes. Thus, it is reasonable to conclude that it was not the intent of Congress that a child remain unnecessarily in foster care while the agency "shops" for a family which might be less suitable but is willing to adopt the child without a subsidy, if it has already found a suitable placement for the child.

QUESTION 3:

Would grounds for a fair hearing exist if the State agency fails to notify or advise adoptive parents of the availability of adoption assistance for a child with special needs?

RESPONSE:

Yes. The very purpose of the title IV-E adoption assistance program is to encourage the adoption of hard-to-place children. State notification to potential adoptive parents about its existence is an intrinsic part of the program and the incentive for adoption that was intended by Congress. Thus, notifying potential adoptive parents is the State agency's responsibility in its administration of the title IV-E adoption assistance program. Accordingly, the State agency's failure to notify the parents may be considered an "extenuating circumstance" which justifies a fair hearing.

QUESTION 4:

Would grounds for a fair hearing exist if the State agency erroneously determines that a child is ineligible for adoption assistance?

RESPONSE:

Yes. If the basis for denial of adoption assistance is the erroneous determination by the State that the child does not meet the eligibility criteria set forth in section 473 of the Act, the adoptive parents may request a fair hearing under section 471(a)(12) of the Act. If the hearing determines that the State erred in its assessment of the child's eligibility for adoption assistance, the State may reverse the earlier decision to deny benefits under title IV-E.

Appendices

-4-

QUESTION 5:

May a State establish policies defining the factual circumstances which constitute an extenuating circumstance for the purpose of a fair hearing?

RESPONSE:

It is permissible for States to have written guidance regarding the types of situations which would constitute the grounds for a fair hearing in order to assist fair hearing officers. However, State policies may not define the grounds for a fair hearing more narrowly than Federal policy. (See 45 CFR 205.10, ACYF-PIQ-83-4, dated October 26, 1983, and ACYF-PIQ-88-06, dated December 2, 1988, for guidance.) The types of situations which would constitute grounds for a fair hearing include: (1) relevant facts regarding the child, the biological family or child's background are known and not presented to the adoptive parents prior to the legalization of the adoption; (2) denial of assistance based upon a means test of the adoptive family; (3) erroneous determination by the State that a child is ineligible for adoption assistance; and (4) failure by the State agency to advise adoptive parents of the availability of adoption assistance.

If applicants or recipients of financial benefits or service programs under titles IV-B or IV-E believe that they have been wrongly denied financial assistance or excluded from a service program, they have a right to a hearing. It is the responsibility of the fair hearing officer to determine whether extenuating circumstances exist and whether the applicant or recipient was wrongly denied eligibility.

QUESTION 6:

May a State agency change its eligibility determination and provide adoption assistance based upon extenuating circumstances without requiring the applicant to obtain a favorable ruling in a fair hearing?

RESPONSE:

No. However, if the State and the parents are in agreement, a trial-type evidentiary hearing would not be necessary. The undisputed documentary evidence could be presented to the

-5-

fair hearing officer for his or her review and determination on
the written record.

QUESTION 7:

Who has the burden of proving extenuating circumstances and
adoption assistance eligibility at a fair hearing?

RESPONSE:

The Federal statute does not address the point explicitly. We
would expect States to conclude that the adoptive parents have
the burden of proving extenuating circumstances and adoption
assistance eligibility at a fair hearing. However, as stated in
the previous response, if the State agency is in agreement that a
family had erroneously been denied benefits, it would be
permissible for the State to provide such facts to the family or
present corroborating facts on behalf of the family to the fair
hearing officer.

QUESTION 8:

After the legalization of an adoption, if a fair hearing
determines that a child has been wrongly denied benefits under
the title IV-E adoption assistance program, what is the earliest
date from which assistance may be provided?

RESPONSE:

Prior to the passage of the Tax Reform Act of 1986, the statute
required that there be an interlocutory or final decree of
adoption prior to receipt of adoption assistance. Therefore,
after the effective date of a State's title IV-E State plan, the
earliest date from which adoption assistance may be provided is
from the time of the interlocutory or final decree of adoption
for those children adopted on or before October 1, 1986. As of
October 1, 1986, with the passage of the Tax Reform Act of 1986,
the requirement that there be an interlocutory decree prior to
providing adoption assistance was rescinded and adoption
assistance payments may begin when the adoption assistance
agreement is signed and the child is placed in the adoptive home.

If a State chooses to pay adoption assistance retroactively from
the earliest date of the child's eligibility in accordance with
Federal and State statutes, regulations and policies, the State

-6-

may claim Federal financial participation for this expenditure.
For cases in which there was no signed adoption assistance
agreement, the earliest date of eligibility would be that of the
interlocutory or final decree for assistance provided before
October 1, 1986, or placement in an adoptive home for assistance
provided after October 1, 1986. States should sign a new
agreement backdated to the earliest date of eligibility for the
child. The two-year restriction in section 1132(a) of the Social
Security Act applies to the date of claim for actual
expenditures, and, thus, would not apply in this situation.

Wade F. Horn, Ph.D.
Commissioner

APPENDIX B:
INFORMATION RESOURCES

Child Welfare League of America, Inc.
440 First Street, NW, Suite 310
Washington, DC 20001–2085
202/638–2952

The Child Welfare League of America (CWLA) is the only privately supported national organization devoting its efforts entirely to the improvement of services for deprived, neglected, abused, and dependent children and youths. CWLA publishes books and other materials on adoption, including nationally recognized standards of practice for adoption agencies and professionals. For a catalog of publications or for information on training opportunities, call the number listed above.

North American Council on Adoptable Children (NACAC)
Raymond, Suite 106
St. Paul, MN 55114–1149
612/644–3036

NACAC has been a national leader in adoption reform efforts over the years and is a good source of information on a wide range of adoption issues, including adoption subsidy, federal policy interpretations, and current adoption legislation. It publishes *Adoptalk* (a quarterly newsletter) and hosts an annual conference for adoptive families and adoption professionals. The agency has recently completed a comprehensive study of adoption subsidy programs.

Zebly Implementation Hotline
Philadelphia, PA
800/523–0000
As a result of the U.S. Supreme Court's decision in *Zebley v. U.S. Department of Health and Human Services* (1990), SSI disability standards for children were revised and made easier to meet. This toll-free number is operated by Community Legal Services in Philadelphia, the legal agency that won the *Zebley* case. The hotline provides information on SSI for children in light of the *Zebley* decision.

About the Author

Tim O'Hanlon, Ph.D., is a leading authority on adoption subsidy policy issues and has been an effective advocate for adoptive families and their children for a number of years. While with the Ohio Department of Human Services, he was instrumental in crafting the policy reforms that allow adoptive families to file appeals for federal adoption assistance and retroactive benefits after a final decree of adoption. He also played a leading role in the creation of Ohio's post-adoption services subsidy program. In partnership with Steve Humerickhouse, formerly of Adoptive Families of America, he recently formed Adoption Advocates, to provide information and guidance to adoptive families in need of post-adoptive services or financial support.

FROM THE
CHILD WELFARE LEAGUE OF AMERICA

ADOPTION —AND— DISCLOSURE

A REVIEW OF THE LAW

By Madelyn DeWoody

*Q*uality adoption practice supports sharing of information so that children with medical, psychological, and developmental problems are placed with families prepared to meet their needs. This report offers a needed overview of the legal developments around disclosure of health and background information in adoption. Part One reviews the major court decisions in this area and summarizes the judicial trends. Part Two reviews statutory law and charts the various ways in which states have defined the nature and scope of duty to disclose nonidentifying information.

1993 / 0–87868–577–4 / Stock #5774
$12.95

To Order:
   CWLA c/o CSSC
   P.O. Box 7816
   300 Raritan Center Parkway
   Edison, NJ   08818
   908 / 225–1900
   Fax 908 / 417–0482

Please specify stock #5774. CWLA pays shipping and handling for prepaid U.S. Orders. Bulk discount policy (not for resale): 10–49 copies 15%; 50 or more copies 20%. Canadian and foreign orders must be prepaid in U.S. funds by international money order. Visa and MasterCard accepted.

NEW from the
Child Welfare League of America

BUILDING
SUPPORT
NETWORKS

A Guide for Parents of Children with Disabilities

by Lizanne Capper

Most parents want to see their children learn and succeed, but those whose children have disabilities find the process difficult and filled with challenges. These parents need information and support. This book explores the many sources of support available for parents of children with mental, emotional, and physical disabilities and guides parents in their search for answers.

1995/0–87868–595–2/Stock #5952 . . . . $18.95

To Order: CWLA c/o CSSC
            P.O. Box 7816 • 300 Raritan Center Parkway
            Edison, NJ   08818
            908/225–1900 • Fax 908/417–0482

Please specify stock #5952. CWLA pays shipping and handling for prepaid U.S. Orders. Bulk discount policy (not for resale): 10–49 copies 15%; 50 or more copies 20%. Canadian and foreign orders must be prepaid in U.S. funds by International money order. Visa and MasterCard accepted.